Below Southwark

the archaeological story

Southwark Council

Published by the London Borough of Southwark for the **Southwark and Lambeth Archaeological Excavation Committee**

This report was commissioned from the Museum of London Archaeology Service by the Southwark and Lambeth Archaeological Excavation Committee, with the support of Southwark Council.

British Library Cataloguing in Publication Data
A CIP catalogue record for this book is available from the British Library

ISBN 0-905849-29-9

For copies of this book, and for trade orders, please contact Laura Schaaf, Secretary, SLAEC, c/o Museum of London, London Wall, London EC2Y 5HN.

Acknowledgements

This book was produced by the Southwark and Lambeth Archaeological Excavation Committee (SLAEC) and the London Borough of Southwark. SLAEC is grateful to London Borough of Southwark for its generous contribution towards the costs of publishing *Below Southwark*.

The text was written by Carrie Cowan of the Museum of London Archaeology Service (MoLAS) with contributions by John Dillon (former Archaeology Officer, London Borough of Southwark) and Kieron Heard (MoLAS) and Monica Kendall who edited the text. Tracy Wellman (MoLAS) designed, typeset and produced the book and Andy Chopping (MoLAS) selected and produced many of the illustrations. Susan Banks (MoLAS) drew the borough maps; Jane Sandoe and Jon Sygrave (MoLAS) prepared the plan of Bermonsey Abbey. The reconstruction of Roman London on page 13 is by Peter Froste. The newspaper cuttings on page 31 are reproduced courtesy of The Times (©Times Newspapers Ltd, 1989 – author Simon Tait, photographer Chris Harris, 16 May 1989) and The Daily Telegraph (©The Daily Telegraph, 1989).

Thanks are due to staff of MoLAS and Southwark's Local Studies Library who provided much information, to members of the Committee for their comments on the text and to Sarah Gibson (the London Borough of Southwark's Senior Archaeology Officer), Peter Hinton and Councillor Dermot McInerney who oversaw the project. Thanks are also due to the specialist advisors for their comments, Simon Blatherwick, John Clark, Jonathan Cotton, Stephen Humphrey and Harvey Sheldon.

Front cover
Above: one of Peckham Square's mosaic sculptures by Duncan Hooson, with the new Peckham Library (architects Alsop and Stormer) which opened in spring 2000
Below: a mid 2nd-century mosaic, discovered during excavations at Mayor Sworders Arches, possibly part of the floor of an important public building
Photographs & montage by Andy Chopping

Back cover
Tudor coins from the site of the Rose Theatre

southwark

Contents

Foreword

During the last quarter century, the regeneration of north Southwark has resulted in many archaeological investigations that have shed light on the rich archaeological heritage of the borough. Before this programme of regeneration began we knew that Southwark had an important medieval and later history, but we knew little of its important prehistoric and Roman past. Archaeological investigations were undertaken primarily by committed amateurs, working in their spare time with few resources to aid their research. There were still many occasions during the 1960s and 1970s when archaeologists had to watch helplessly as precious evidence for Southwark's past was destroyed without record. During the 1970s and 1980s a growing band of professional archaeologists, guided by the Southwark and Lambeth Archaeological Excavation Committee (SLAEC), worked with developers to investigate sites properly. They made startling discoveries, and they started to put together the jigsaw pieces of Southwark's past.

Since 1990 archaeology has been emphasised as an important part of the planning process, and Southwark Council is committed to the preservation, investigation and display of the borough's archaeological heritage. The Council's Archaeology Officer ensures that wherever possible Southwark's regeneration results in the preservation of our past, and allows Southwark's residents to learn about the results of archaeological excavations.

From these endeavours we now know far more about the borough's history. Archaeologists have shown us how the process of regeneration has been going on for centuries, how Southwark's residents have shaped their environment, and how new peoples have blended with existing cultures to produce a rich and changing mixture of communities. The Council is pleased to contribute to this book, which illustrates an archaeology every Southwark resident should be proud of.

Councillor Stephanie Elsy
Leader of Southwark Council

SLAEC in early days

As Chair of SLAEC I am delighted to welcome you to *Below Southwark: the archaeological story*. This book summarises the results of investigations in the borough by both amateur and professional archaeologists. SLAEC (initially SAEC) was established in 1962 by the London and Middlesex and the Surrey Archaeological Societies to coordinate archaeological work in the borough (later extending its remit to Lambeth). In time it employed its own archaeological team, which was later integrated into the Museum of London. The Committee continues to play an active role in guiding and contributing to research and excavation in the boroughs. The Committee comprises officers and members of both Councils, and archaeologists and historians – both professional and amateur – from a wide range of backgrounds. It seeks to promote a greater awareness of the archaeological heritage of Southwark and Lambeth. That is why SLAEC has published this book.

Professor Clive Orton
Chair of the Southwark and Lambeth Archaeological Excavation Committee (SLAEC)

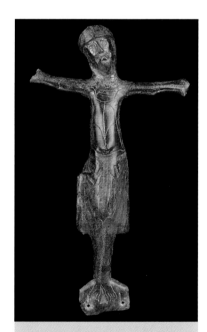
This 13th-century figure of Christ crucified was found at Bermondsey Abbey. Decorated with enamel, it was probably once attached to an altar or processional cross and may have been made at Limoges in France

Neolithic flint axe from the Bricklayers Arms excavations

Roman brooch, probably from France, in the form of a couching hare inlaid with black niello decoration. It was found at the former Courage's Brewery in Park Street

A Tudor cannonball of Portland Stone found at London Bridge City on Tooley Street

Introduction

This book tells how archaeologists have uncovered the story of Southwark. It is a story that covers thousands of years of major changes in its landscape and society. Using the latest archaeological discoveries and illustrated by many photographs, drawings and old maps, we shall catch a glimpse of the lives of the past peoples who once lived and worked in the area we now call Southwark.

Our story begins with hunter-gatherers on the Old Kent Road. It tells of the first farmers in Bermondsey. With the arrival of the Romans, Southwark grew into an urban centre, traces of which have been found under modern streets and offices and during the construction of the Jubilee Line Extension. In medieval times there were two royal residences, as well as a priory in Southwark and an abbey at Bermondsey. The 16th and 17th centuries saw Bankside develop into an entertainment centre with theatres known to Shakespeare, such as the Rose and the Globe.

Later, Southwark became increasingly industrialised, with leatherworking, clay tobacco pipemaking, shipyards and potteries. The book ends with the arrival of the canals and railways in the 19th century – but the story goes on as Southwark's people enter a new millennium, leaving their mark for archaeologists in the future.

The London Borough of Southwark

The modern London Borough of Southwark is roughly triangular-shaped stretching over five miles from the Thames to Crystal Palace and Sydenham Hill.

The historic centre or focus of the borough lies at London Bridge and The Borough with the traditionally industrial areas of Bermondsey and the docklands of Rotherhithe to the east. Much of the story therefore concentrates on this historic core as this is where most of Southwark's past inhabitants lived and worked. To the south are the suburbs, originally the villages, of Newington, Walworth and Camberwell. Further south are Peckham, Nunhead and Dulwich.

This is a diverse terrain. Much of the borough is situated within the gravel-terraced valley of the River Thames. In the north of the borough, the land is low-lying where it fronts the river and has been subject to flooding. To the south there is a ridge of higher ground which roughly corresponds to the line of the Old Kent Road. Further to the south, towards the tip of the triangle, the ground is higher still towards Dulwich and Peckham.

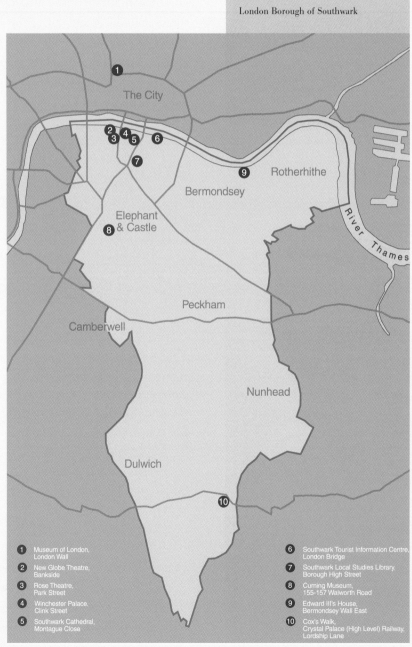

London Borough of Southwark

1 Museum of London,
London Wall

2 New Globe Theatre,
Bankside

3 Rose Theatre,
Park Street

4 Winchester Palace,
Clink Street

5 Southwark Cathedral,
Montague Close

6 Southwark Tourist Information Centre,
London Bridge

7 Southwark Local Studies Library,
Borough High Street

8 Cuming Museum,
155-157 Walworth Road

9 Edward III's House,
Bermondsey Wall East

10 Cox's Walk,
Crystal Palace (High Level) Railway,
Lordship Lane

What is archaeology?

Archaeological excavations have produced a wealth of information and artefacts that tell us how people lived. Much of our knowledge of Southwark's history is due to the work of archaeologists. Archaeologists discover exactly what took place throughout time and how this affected the environment and the population. But what is archaeology and how is it carried out?

Archaeology is the study of the past through its physical remains. Some archaeology is above the ground like the remains of the medieval hall of Winchester Palace which can be seen in Clink Street. But many traces of human activity and events often lie buried below the modern buildings and streets of Southwark. Over the centuries the ground level has increased by up to 3 metres as new buildings have been constructed over the demolished remains of earlier ones. It is the job of the archaeologist to excavate and record these remains prior to their destruction by redevelopment.

Each archaeological layer, such as a layer of dumped rubbish or a floor, or archaeological feature, such as a wall or a posthole, is exposed, cleaned and recorded before removal or reburial, and the artefacts and samples from the layer or feature are collected. The excavation continues layer after layer until archaeologists reach the ground surface that existed before humans arrived in Southwark.

When the excavation is complete, the records, samples and finds are studied and a report is published. In this way a record of what was once below ground survives.

The samples taken from the layers and features may contain traces of plant and animal remains such as pollen and bones. This information can be used to reconstruct the landscape and the local environment at that time, and yield information on what the people's diet was like. The artefacts, such as broken pottery and leather shoes, will help to date the layers and features, and tell us how the people lived.

In this way, sequences of human activity representing the prehistory (that is, before written records survive) and history of Southwark are recovered from small trenches or larger areas available for archaeological excavation in Southwark's redevelopment programmes.

An archaeologist surveying on the Thames foreshore in Southwark at the Millennium Bridge excavations

Archaeologists share the construction site beneath Borough High Street, dodging the electricity cables and water and telecom services that can be seen suspended beneath the road deck

Specialists such as this conservator clean and analyse finds from excavations

Prehistoric lives and landscapes

Southwark's prehistoric landscape

Archaeological excavations have shown that there have been people in Southwark for at least 10,000 years since the Mesolithic (or Middle Stone Age) period.

At that time Southwark's environment was totally different from that of today. In the south of the borough, along the gravel terraces where the land is hillier, Southwark was a forest of pine and birch roamed by red deer and wild cattle or 'aurochs', which were hunted by these early people.

North Southwark, however, was low-lying and marshy. The River Thames was much wider and consisted of many small channels surrounding higher areas of sandy islands. These sandy islands would have been attractive to the people. People would have found these areas an important source of food, providing an ideal location for hunting animals, gathering plants and for fishing. This is why people from all periods used this rather wet area.

The River Thames looked quite different in the Neolithic (New Stone Age) period. Under a pontoon to be constructed on the Thames foreshore near **New Globe Walk**, Bankside, archaeologists found Neolithic alder trees. They show that the river was lower in the Neolithic period than it is today – perhaps as much as 5 metres lower. The sea levels and thus the river levels rose generally throughout the prehistoric period flooding some of the lowest islands and making them uninhabitable.

During the Neolithic and the Bronze Age much of the woodland was felled to make way for fields in the north of the borough. There was less clearance in the south which remained forested until well into the 18th century. This north–south split is probably due to differences in terrain and soils. The sandy islands had light, well-drained soils well suited to early farming, and the River Thames acted as a highway making the north of the borough more accessible. The south of the borough had heavier, less well-drained clay soils which would not have been attractive to the early farmers.

Excavating flints found at the B&Q store on the Old Kent Road

The hunter-gatherers
Palaeolithic (Old Stone Age) 500,000-9000 BC
Mesolithic (Middle Stone Age) 9000-4000 BC

Early farmers
Neolithic (New Stone Age) and
Early Bronze Age (4000–1500 BC)

Settled farming communities
Middle Bronze Age (1500–650 BC) and
Iron Age (650 BC to AD 43)

The B&Q store on the Old Kent Road/Bowles Road. The shop lies on the site where hunter-gatherers once made flint tools

Flints found at the Bricklayers Arms site

Archaeologists draw a plan of the prehistoric pits at the former Courage's Brewery site in Park Street

The hunter-gatherers

The Mesolithic hunter's raw material was flint, skilfully chipped and shaped into blades, arrowheads and other tools.

Under the **B&Q store** on the **Old Kent Road** archaeologists found a place where Southwark's hunter-gatherer population made flint tools. It was on a sandy island overlooking the now buried **River Peck** and close to the shoreline of a large lake which existed then. Over 1700 flint artefacts were found, including tools such as scrapers for cutting animal hides, and hammerstones. This was probably a temporary camp and is a rare and important find. Very few such camps have been found in the London region. More flint tools were found at **Marlborough Grove** 200 metres to the north.

Some hunter-gatherer tools were made of antlers from red deer. An antler mattock or pick found near **Bankside Power Station**, now the Tate Gallery of Modern Art, could have been used for digging.

Early farmers

The era of the hunter-gatherers gradually drew to a close during the Neolithic and Early Bronze Age as people began to live in more permanent settlements where they used a new invention, pottery, for cooking and storing food. They also started to domesticate animals and to plant crops. The advent of farming in Britain was almost certainly as a result of trade and communication with people from the Continent, where farming had begun much earlier. It would have been a very gradual change, with hunting and gathering still playing an important role.

Two fire pits or hearths containing burnt clay were found on the river's edge at the former Courage's Brewery site in **Park Street**. A flint arrowhead and some small fragments of animal bone show that people may have been camping here. Archaeologists found one sandy island which had been settled: here flint scrapers and flint knife blades were found along with postholes of circular huts. This island was in the **Hopton Street** area close to Blackfriars Bridge.

Excavations at the **B&Q** site in the **Old Kent Road** also revealed a scatter of flint tools, including a leaf-shaped arrowhead, which indicates that the area of the earlier camp continued to be a favoured spot. Flint tools have also been found in the area of **Guy's Hospital**, on what had once been a sandy island, and in **Hanover Park** in Peckham.

Neolithic pottery has been found by archaeologists on several sites in Southwark. Some broken pieces of pottery were found in **St Thomas Street**. It was decorated with impressions made from bird bones and twisted cord.

Neolithic pottery from the Jubilee Line Extension excavations

The first use of metal appeared alongside a new style of pottery, Beaker pots. These drinking vessels have been found in many parts of north-west Europe; they were brought to England by traders but are rare in the London area. The beakers are thought to have held an alcoholic honeyed drink made from fermented flowers, similar to mead. In **Southwark Street** a deliberately buried deposit was found which included four flint tools and fragments of Beaker pottery. It was the first such find in central London.

A complete Beaker bowl was found buried in a small pit at **Hopton Street**. This may also have been deliberately buried – perhaps as an offering. Ceremony and ritual were important parts of these peoples' lives.

The Beaker bowl found at Hopton Street
Photo © Pre-Construct Archaeology

Metalwork, both bronze and iron, has been recovered from the Thames and its tributaries. A bronze axe, a complete circular shield now in the British Museum, a bronze leaf-shaped spearhead, a potin (tin-rich bronze) coin, a gold coin and a coin of the Iron Age king Cunobelin have been found in the river in the London Bridge area, many of them during dredging in the 19th century. Some river objects may have been washed out from riverside settlements, but some of the larger objects, such as the axe and spearhead, may well have formed part of the already centuries-old tradition of ritually depositing valuable items in the river – as offerings to the gods.

At the site of former **Phoenix Wharf, Jamaica Road**, archaeologists found a rectangular pit, perhaps originally clay-lined, containing burnt flints. A small mound was found next to the pit, where the charcoal debris had been piled from repeated use of the pit. A line of stakes probably formed a windbreak. A separate group of postholes formed a small hut or shelter. The pit may have been used for cooking, perhaps for communal or ritual feasting. Water inside the pit may have been heated up by placing hot pebbles in it and food would have cooked by being boiled.

The cooking pit found at Phoenix Wharf

This pit was located on an island which was still used in the medieval period and then known as Horsleydown. Another cooking pit was found buried under peat at **Tanner Street** in the yard of the old Sarson's Vinegar factory.

Because of the low-lying character of north Southwark, prehistoric remains became buried under flood deposits. Archaeologists discovered ard marks (from primitive ploughs) that were still recognisable in the ground at **Wolseley Street** and **Phoenix Wharf** near Jamaica Road. They were buried 3 metres below today's street level. It is rare for prehistoric plough marks to survive. The farmers used wooden ards to break undisturbed ground, loosening it for cultivation with hoes and spades. Further traces of ard marks have subsequently been found at **Lafone Street**, close by, and at **Hopton Street**.

The criss-cross patterns in the ground at the bottom of the trench at Wolseley Street were made by an ard (a primitive plough)

An ard plough being used in Bermondsey

A prehistoric platform found at the former Bricklayers' Arms Goods Yard. The timbers had survived because they were sealed by up to 2 metres of flood clay which would have created the anaerobic (airless) conditions necessary for timber preservation

Many archaeological sites in Southwark have revealed peat in the areas between the islands. The presence of peat means that the river level had temporarily fallen and the areas were becoming marshland where signs of human activity might be found. At **Canada Water, Surrey Quays Road**, peat deposits contained a large split tree and red deer antlers. In **Southwark Park**, a bronze spearhead was found within the peats.

In one marshy area, at the former **Bricklayers' Arms Goods Yard** in Bermondsey, archaeologists found a platform of alder, willow and birch. The platform was either a landing stage for boats or a useful surface from which to fish and hunt, to supplement the produce of the farms.

A trackway was laid across the marsh to the east of the Bricklayers' Arms site, at **Bramcote Grove** near **South Bermondsey Station**. It was made of oak logs held in place by sharpened alder stakes, some of which showed the blade marks left by bronze axes. The trackway led from the high land to the south to Bermondsey, which at the time was an island surrounded by marshes. The route was obviously important as its construction would have taken a good deal of organisation and hard work and shows that the people regularly needed to get from the high dry areas down to the marshlands and the river.

The Bramcote Grove trackway was laid across the marsh to provide access from the high ground to the south to Bermondsey island in the north. Flooding may still have occurred and the trackway may have been used seasonally

How the Bramcote Grove trackway may have looked. The vegetation in the picture is based on pollen and trees found by archaeologists

In the Bronze Age people were as likely to be cremated as buried in the ground. Often their ashes were buried in mounds, or round barrows, surrounded by a circular ditch. One such barrow was discovered at former **Fennings Wharf**, now **No. 1 London Bridge**, in a location that, in the Bronze Age, would have occupied a prominent position. No trace of the mound remained as it had been flattened by the foundations of a 19th-century warehouse, but in the ditch, archaeologists found spreads of cremated bone. The cremations came from the remains of at least five people, four of whom were children.

Part of the ring ditch found at former Fennings Wharf

A decorated antler tine (left) dated to the Iron Age may have belonged to a pony bridle; the piece of polished bone (above) may have been used as an archer's wristguard

Settled farming communities

During the middle of the Bronze Age and into the Iron Age, settlement and agriculture became more intensive.

In Southwark, the people lived in small farming communities. There was still nothing that could be described as an urban centre in Southwark, although there is a possibility that this remains to be discovered. The population grew, but at the same time the river levels rose, and some of the islands disappeared under water.

The remaining sandy islands were now used for farms. On the Bermondsey island archaeologists found Iron Age pottery at both **Abbey Street** and **Grange Road**, as well as a loom weight from a weaving loom. One exciting find was a piece of antler decorated with a ring and dot pattern which may have been part of a pony bridle.

On the most northerly island in **Southwark Street**, archaeologists found stakeholes and small linear and semicircular gullies, probably for timber structures. One was circular and may have been a hut or outhouse for the farm. Pottery was found at **St Thomas Street**.

Another settlement was found in **Tooley Street**. This farm was located on the Horsleydown island. Pottery, rubbish pits, ditches and postholes were discovered. There were also charred cereal grains, including primitive wheat and barley. The farm probably existed sometime between the 1st century BC and the 1st century AD, so it may have lasted into the early Roman period.

Carefully excavating the prehistoric pottery found at Tooley Street

Reconstruction of prehistoric north Southwark

The Romans in Southwark

Roman roads and settlement

Looking at Southwark today, it is initially hard to see what impact the 350 years of Roman occupation has had, but in fact the founding of Southwark and its early importance is almost entirely due to the Romans.

The Roman invasion of Britain in AD 43 was quickly followed by the construction of Watling Street – a major road between Canterbury and London. Watling Street was on the line of modern **Tabard Street** and the **Old Kent Road**.

Excavations in 1990 on the Old Kent Road uncovered a 40-metre length of Roman road, probably Watling Street. The road was made of gravel and only the lower levels survived. It was up to 14 metres wide with ditches either side of it

> **The Roman invasion**
>
> The first military contact between Rome and southern Britain occurred in 55 and 54 BC when Julius Caesar invaded during his conquest of Gaul. His account tells us that he crossed the Thames in pursuit of Cassivelaunus, leader of the Britons, although where this crossing was is unknown.
>
> After this invasion Britain remained independent of Rome for nearly a century, although literature and archaeological discoveries in southern Britain suggest considerable diplomatic and trading activity.
>
> In AD 43 the Roman Emperor Claudius invaded Britain, ostensibly because he was asked to intervene in affairs here by 'a certain Berikos', presumably an influential tribal leader.

Watling Street was linked to the Roman bridge approach road which followed the line of **Borough High Street**. The road crossed the River Thames on probably the first bridge to have been built across the river. It was located a few metres downstream from the present-day London Bridge. The position of the Roman bridge was determined by Southwark's landscape. Much of north Southwark was still low-lying and consisted of a series of sandy islands surrounded by mud flats and intersected by small channels of the Thames. At the point where the river was crossed there was a sandy island in the marsh which provided firm ground and the shortest crossing to London.

The modern Old Kent Road generally follows the ancient line of Roman Watling Street

A surviving fragment of the Roman road near Southwark Cathedral. The road has been cut through by later medieval pits

Photo © Pre-Construct Archaeology

On the north bank of the river the land was higher and here the Roman town of Londinium that underlies the City of London was built.

It was not easy to build the roads across the marsh but the Romans managed it by traversing the higher sandy islands. Archaeologists found the Roman bridge approach road under **Borough High Street**. Where it crossed the marsh, the Romans had built a foundation of oak and alder logs to stop the road from sinking. The top was surfaced with gravel and often became worn and had to be resurfaced.

The land in Borough High Street has been much built up since then and the Roman roads lie nearly 3 metres below today's streets.

Another Roman road, Stane Street, joined Watling Street somewhere in the vicinity of today's **Borough Underground Station**. Its route is followed by **Newington Causeway** and **Kennington Park Road**, leading south to the Roman town of Chichester and the south coast.

A second major road was found near **Southwark Cathedral** and may have linked the Roman bridge to a crossing further upstream, perhaps near Westminster.

Reconstruction of Roman Southwark on the sandy islands at the southern (left) end of the bridge

Smaller roads linked the main highways to the buildings. One was found under the Jubilee Line Extension ticket hall at **Borough High Street**; wheel ruts made by carts were still visible in the road surface.

The Roman settlement was quickly established. Archaeological investigations over the last 30 years of the 20th century continually added to our knowledge and understanding of its layout and development. For many years it was thought that Southwark was simply a small suburb to the main Roman settlement on the north bank of the Thames. However, an extensive series of excavations in the 1980s and 1990s has changed our views. It is now apparent that Southwark was an major settlement and an integral part of Londinium.

The side road found at Jubilee Line Extension ticket hall at Borough High Street. The wheel ruts made by carts were still visible

Southwark was the largest and most complex of the known roadside settlements along the roads approaching Londinium, occupying an estimated area of some 20–24 hectares in the early 2nd century. Finds of military equipment and coins of the Emperor Claudius suggest a military influence in the early settlement, but later Southwark may have shared Londinium's functions as the administrative centre of Roman Britain.

In Londinium and Southwark archaeologists often uncover a layer of burnt debris from Roman buildings destroyed by fire dated to around the middle of the 1st century AD. The destruction is likely to have been caused as a result of the rebellion of Boudica, Queen of the East Anglia Iceni tribe. Literary sources tell us that her tribe together with the Trinovantes of Essex sacked and burned Londinium and also much of north Southwark in AD 60 in an attempt to drive the Roman armies out of Britain.

Some fire debris was found during excavations at **Borough High Street**, part of the Jubilee Line Extension. Here a 60 metre long expanse of Roman buildings had been burned. After the rebellion was suppressed it is likely that rebuilding occurred quickly.

Jubilee Line Extension ticket hall at Borough High Street

Bronze statue on Victoria Embankment of Queen Boudica and her daughters in a chariot, unveiled in 1902. Prince Albert lent his horses as models to the sculptor Thomas Thornycroft

Roman buildings

The settlement within north Southwark grew up along the two major roads and probably stretched as far south as where **St George's Church** stands today.

Most houses were rectangular but some of the earliest houses were circular following on from the Iron Age traditional roundhouses. One house was found on the former **Courage's Brewery** site in **Park Street**. Another roundhouse was found at former **Toppings Wharf**, now offices at **No. 1 London Bridge**. This house contained metalworking hearths and the floor was littered with metalworking debris, mainly iron slag, with some bronze.

Buildings were mostly made of clay with a timber frame and a thatched or tiled roof. The floors were often earth or clay though the more prestigious buildings had mortar and tile floors.

At the former **Courage's Brewery** site archaeologists found overlying the remains of one building, a clay floor of another later building. An amphora had been placed under the floor perhaps as a ceremonial offering for the building, a little like laying a foundation stone today. Some of the clay walls survived, dividing the building into four rooms. The walls were decorated with painted maroon plaster with black splashes.

Outside the building were two timber-lined wells in a yard for use by the occupants. Nearby was a half-cellared building made of clay bricks. It had a tiled floor on which a burnt offering had been placed – or maybe a storage deposit of barley had caught fire.

A piece of mosaic from the Jubilee Line Extension excavations

A major achievement of the 1980s and 1990s has been the discovery of substantial stone buildings in Roman Southwark. These larger buildings were furnished with mosaic and mortar floors, finely painted wall plaster, tiled roofs and underfloor heating systems.

The burnt tiled floor in a cellared building found under the former Courage's Brewery at Park Street

An archaeologist cleans the painted wall plaster on a clay and timber building

A 2nd-century stone building found under Borough High Street

One of these was a prominent Roman riverfront building found under medieval Winchester Palace in **Clink Street**. Five of the seven identified rooms had been fitted with hypocausts (underfloor heating). This heated suite of rooms may have been a bath-house.

A fine piece of painted wall plaster had collapsed face down but archaeologists have pieced it together to reveal a scene of columns decorated with garlands around a figure of Cupid holding a plate. The design was in a rich colour scheme of green, yellow and red. It is now in the Museum of London.

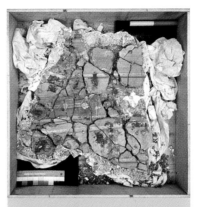

Fragments of Roman painted wall plaster from the Winchester Palace excavations were carefully removed from the site

A clue to the use of the Roman building at Winchester Palace was found in the stokehole of one of its hypocausted rooms. This was a broken marble inscription of early 3rd-century date which listed the names of soldiers within cohorts. It is possible that this was a building dedication put up by military builders or residents in honour of the family of the reigning emperor

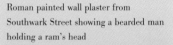

The painted wall plaster after cleaning and restoration

Roman painted wall plaster from Southwark Street showing a bearded man holding a ram's head

Another large courtyard building was found in Southwark Street and may have been an inn or *mansio*, a building used for overnight accommodation for government officials carrying goods and dispatches. One suite of rooms was decorated with painted wall plaster showing a bearded man holding a ram's head, perhaps part of a ritual sacrifice.

A large amphora found in a Roman building during the Jubilee Line Extension excavations. The building may have been a warehouse for storing the goods shipped into Southwark

Trade and industry

That Roman Southwark was an important centre of riverborne trade is being established by archaeological study. There are a number of sites in north Southwark where evidence exists for the construction of timber waterfronts or revetments to the edges of river channels. Archaeologists found one such revetment constructed of posts and wattle at **64–70 Borough High Street**. The purpose of these revetments was to protect the low-lying land from erosion and to render the marshy land habitable for construction. The waterfronts allowed for boats to be moored, and loading and trading to take place.

Near **Guy's Hospital** a wooden jetty, a walkway and a series of revetments from the 1st to the 4th century were found in a watercourse that once ran into the main river. The 2nd-century revetment was constructed of posts with planks attached and over 30 metres were excavated. It included raking braces and a series of rubbing posts which would have protected the main structure from the barges and boats. Boats used the smaller watercourses and channels to collect and deliver goods. The remains of a large boat, a flat-bottomed lighter, were found submerged in the channel. It now lies preserved under buildings.

Close to the channel edge a small timber tank dated to the 3rd century was uncovered, possibly for storing oysters or fish before selling on.

Sometimes the dry land was protected with embankments. Such an embankment was found on the former **Courage's Brewery** site. Stakes were driven into the flooded area and then clay was packed around them to create a bank.

On the same site there was a warehouse made entirely of timber. It lay close to the river and was thus ideally located for trade and supply. It was sunk into the ground and would have been cool and damp – ideal conditions for the storage of wines and food.

Reconstruction of the timber warehouse

Courage's Brewery timber warehouse. This is a remarkably well-preserved building and is a unique find in Roman Britain

Large quantities of amphorae – Roman storage jars – were found inside one building on the **Jubilee Line Extension** excavations. They were used for transporting commodities such as black olives in syrup, wine, fish sauce and alum (used for fixing dyes to textiles), and had come from Spain, France and Italy. An exceptional find from **Winchester Palace** was an amphora with surviving contents that included Spanish mackerel bones. It was inscribed with the word *liquamen* (fish sauce) and was produced by Lucius Tettius Africanus of *Antipolis* (modern Antibes) and imported from the Mediterranean. Pots made in Cologne have been found in a well at the former **Hibernia Wharf.**

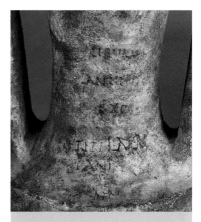

Inscribed amphora from the Winchester Palace excavations

Also on the former **Courage's Brewery** site, archaeologists found hearths that had been used for metalworking: iron smithing and copper-alloy casting. Tools, nails, studs, personal ornaments and vessels were produced. Antlerworking was also carried out. Red deer antlers were made into combs, buttons and knife handles.

Some buildings were houses but others were used as shops. Archaeologists found a blacksmith's workshop under the Jubilee Line Extension station at **London Bridge.** Another building contained charred cereal grain and may have been a bakery. Large amounts of chopped and sawn cattle bones were found in a nearby shop, perhaps a butcher's. Skulls of lambs were found in **Borough High Street** and had probably been slaughtered nearby. It is not hard to imagine the approach road hemmed in by shops with traders plying their wares to the locals and the travellers heading for the bridge into the city.

Roman pots made in Cologne, from a well at the former Hibernia Wharf, Montague Close. The pots in the foreground are decorated with hunting scenes

Farming was carried out to the south of the main Roman settlement. Field boundaries, drainage ditches and remains of timber buildings have been found on the **Old Kent Road** on the outskirts of the main settlement. A rubbish pit was found at **Lisford Street** just to the north of **Peckham Town Square**, and pottery, tile and coins were found in the **Rotherhithe** area.

Reconstruction drawing of a blacksmith hammering on an anvil

Metalworking hearths were found at the former Courage's Brewery site

Religion and burial

In the crypt under **Southwark Cathedral**, a group of sculptures were discovered thrown into a well. They had originally come from a mausoleum or shrine. There was a statue of a hunter god with a dog and a deer, part of a sea god in Greek marble, probably Neptune or Oceanus, and a sandstone figure of a Genius, a god of an area of spiritual significance. As these figures were of religious significance, it may not be coincidental that a Christian church was later founded on the same spot.

Burials in the Roman period were generally restricted to areas outside the settlement. Some bodies were placed in wooden coffins and buried in the ground (these are called inhumations); others were burned and the ashes placed in a pot and buried (cremations). Burials have been found in Southwark alongside the major roads where the funerary monuments would easily have been seen.

Between **Tabard Street** and **Great Dover Street**, alongside Roman Watling Street, archaeologists have found a number of inhumation and cremation burials of adults and children. Some of the burials were inside a walled cemetery and were laid around a central mortar plinth which may have been the base of a sarcophagus or a monument. There was also a small masonry building which could have been a mausoleum. Fragments of carved stone from funerary monuments were found, including a stone head of a river god. A cremation pit contained a large number of lamps and pots.

Intaglio (gemstone) from a Roman ring found during excavations at the B&Q store site on the Old Kent Road. It depicts a fabulous creature composed of a cock, a horse and a Silenus mask

A Roman burial at Great Dover Street

At **Swan Street**, on the west side of **Great Dover Street**, 15 wells were found close together and many contained complete pots found at the base of the wells which might have some ritual meaning. In one well a male skeleton was found and may have been deliberately placed there.

Head of a river god from Great Dover Street

Another cemetery was found at **Bermondsey**. Three cremations within an enclosing ditch were found at **Cherry Garden Street** and belonged to a small, rural type of Roman cemetery. Each cremation was placed in, or associated with, a pot, which was within a pit. The pots had been broken, probably in antiquity.

A limestone finial in the shape of a pine cone from a mausoleum at Great Dover Street

Later Roman burials have been found in an arc stretching from **Park Street** to **Southwark Street**, **Redcross Way** and round to **Guy's Hospital** area. Grave goods are rare though one young woman at **Southwark Street** was buried with a pottery vessel at her head and jet and bone ornaments at her waist. Another woman was buried with chicken bones between her legs and this may have been intended for food in the afterlife. These burials are thought to be of a late 4th-century date and, as they were inside the Roman settlement, where burials were not normally allowed, they may indicate that the settlement was becoming smaller at this time. Perhaps parts of the settlement had been abandoned. This might have been due to attacks from Saxons across the North Sea. The Roman government in Britain ceased in AD 411.

A sequence of square and circular wells from the 1st and 2nd centuries AD. A male skeleton was found in one shaft, head down, with several pottery vessels accompanying it.

Photos © Pre-Construct Archaeology

Saxon and medieval Southwark

Attacks and invaders

After the end of the period of Roman rule in Britain, new settlers crossed the sea from north Germany. So far archaeologists have found few traces of these early Saxon settlers in Southwark, though villages like **Peckham** may have had their origins in this period. Saxon pottery has been found during excavations in **Peckham High Street**.

A large monastic church or 'minster' might have been established on the island at **Bermondsey** as early as the 7th or 8th century. The place-name Bermondsey is of Saxon origin meaning 'Beormund's isle'; Beormund was perhaps one of the first English settlers to occupy and farm here. Loom weights and two silver coins dated to the Saxon period were found by archaeologists at Bermondsey as well as a large ditch which had been lined with timber, presumably to act as a drain.

Southwark grew as a response to Viking attacks on England in the 9th century, when it was probably one of a network of fortified towns known as 'burhs'. In the 10th and 11th centuries Southwark played a vital role in the defence of England. Together with the city of London, Southwark controlled the passage up the River Thames, thus blocking the invasion route.

We do not know how long the Roman bridge survived, or when it was replaced. Archaeologists found the southern abutment of a succession of timber bridges at former **Fennings Wharf**, now **No. 1 London Bridge**. One of the bridges was dated by dendrochronology (tree-ring dating) to the Late Saxon period of late 10th- or early 11th-century date.

The Saxon ditch from Bermondsey Abbey

One document, the Olaf Saga, recounts how in 1013 the bridge was attacked successfully by the Viking Olaf Haroldson (later king of Norway), who went on to capture Southwark from the occupying Danes. The Saga calls Southwark *Suthvirki* and describes it as 'a great trading place,' defended by 'large ditches' with a road and a rampart constructed of 'wood, stone and turf' and defended by 'a great army'. As yet archaeologists have found no trace of the ramparts but a large ditch, over 4 metres wide, was found at the former **Hibernia Wharf** in **Montague Close**. It was of early 11th-century date and it is likely that it formed part of Southwark's defensive earthworks. A Saxon paddle from a boat was found in the ditch. Saxon boat timbers have also been found at former Fennings Wharf.

The Saxon paddle at former Hibernia Wharf, Montague Close

In May 1016 the Southwark bridgehead was again defended, this time against King Cnut, who bypassed it by reputedly digging a new channel for his ships through the marshes and creeks of Southwark, thus avoiding an attack on the actual bridge. The course of Cnut's channel is unknown and indeed sounds an unlikely venture.

The army of William the Conqueror attacked and burned Southwark at the time of the Norman Conquest of 1066. Domesday Book of 1086 was commissioned by William as an inventory for taxation purposes and lists many of the medieval manorial estates. For Southwark, the book lists at least 50 households, a minster church (probably on the site of the present **Southwark Cathedral**), St Mary Overie dock, a trading shore where boats pulled up to sell goods, and a herring fishery.

Excavations at Fennings Wharf. The archaeologist on the left of the picture is standing on the 12th-century bridge abutment whilst the archaeologist on the right of the picture collects samples from the elm piles under the 15th-century bridge abutment for dendrochronological analysis (tree-ring dating)

London Bridge

Roman Southwark developed because of its important location at the southern approach to the bridge across the Thames. During the medieval period Southwark continued to develop and thrive for the same reason: until the construction of Westminster Bridge in 1738–50 London Bridge was the only point of access to the City and Westminster for traffic from the south and was where the roads to the south converged as in Roman times.

In 1176 Peter, chaplain of St Mary Colechurch – one of the City of London churches – began construction of the first stone London Bridge. The bridge had many piers that partly dammed the flow of the Thames. On occasions the weight of ice forming upstream of the piers caused parts of the bridge to collapse. At **Fennings Wharf**, archaeologists uncovered the stone piers of the bridge. The piers had been founded on platforms of rubble reinforced with short timber piles, on which timber baseplates were laid. The walls of the piers were faced with stone and the interior of the piers was filled with rubble.

Detail from Wyngaerde's London panorama of c 1544 showing the buildings on London Bridge. This was the first stone bridge in London across the Thames and was begun in 1176. The houses were demolished in the 18th century, and the bridge was removed in the early 19th century
Ashmolean Museum, Oxford

Thomas Becket (St Thomas the Martyr) was Archbishop of Canterbury from 1162 until his murder in 1170, carried out at the prompting of Henry II. He was immediately hailed as a martyr and thereafter his shrine at Canterbury Cathedral became a place of pilgrimage. This early 15th-century Canterbury souvenir badge was found during excavations at the Jubilee Line Extension

The bridge took over 30 years to build, and was finally completed in the reign of King John. At the Southwark end there was a drawbridge and a large stone gate. On the bridge were houses, shops and a chapel of St Thomas the Martyr.

The medieval riverfront

Erosion and flooding by the Thames were huge problems for the inhabitants of medieval Southwark. Excavations along the riverfront at Southwark have uncovered a series of waterfront structures: from 11th-century timber revetments at **Fennings Wharf**, to stone river walls of the 15th and 16th centuries at **Winchester Palace**. Many of the revetment timbers have been reused and derive from clinker-built boats constructed with overlapping planks. Archaeologists found such a boat at **London Bridge City** in **Tooley Street**. This was a 13th-century rowing galley with three ports for oars and cut-outs for the benches on which the oarsmen sat. It was preserved because its planks had been reused in a wooden fish tank.

The modern roads **Bermondsey Wall East**, **Bermondsey Wall West** and **Rotherhithe Street** probably mark the line of the old river defences. Recently archaeologists found a medieval chalk wall which was part of the river defences at **Adlards Wharf**, Bermondsey Wall West.

Fennings Wharf is now occupied by the grand offices of No. 1 London Bridge

The 13th-century boat timbers found at London Bridge City in Tooley Street

Medieval settlements

In medieval times Southwark was a thriving commercial and manufacturing community. It had a market and (from at least 1444) a fair and was renowned for its numerous taverns which catered for travellers on the main road from London to the south. The best known of these travellers are the Canterbury pilgrims bound for the shrine of Thomas Becket. The famous Tabard Inn from which the pilgrims set out lay on **Borough High Street** until the 1870s, near the present **George Inn** (a late 17th-century inn with part of its galleried courtyard still remaining). Geoffrey Chaucer describes the pilgrimage in *The Canterbury Tales*, written in the late 14th century.

Initially the settlement of Southwark was concentrated around London Bridge, but by the end of the medieval period it had expanded along the riverfront eastwards to **Horsleydown** (in the **Tooley Street** area) and westwards along **Bankside**. To the south it extended along **Borough High Street** as far as **St George's Church**.

There were other medieval settlements in the borough. **Peckham** was included in Domesday Book as Pecheha, meaning 'settlement among the hills'. The hills referred to are probably **Plow Garlick**, **Nunhead** and **Honor Oak**. The village was largely confined to the **High Street** area and the rest of Peckham was rural with market gardens and pasture. The manorial estate of **Dulwich** was part of Bermondsey Abbey's lands in the medieval period (see below). **Camberwell**, **Peckham**, **Walworth** and **Kennington** are among the villages mentioned in Domesday Book of 1086 (a hide is a land unit roughly equivalent to 120 acres; a virgate is the quarter of a hide).

Recently some of these field systems have been examined by archaeologists. In **Peckham High Street** a pit containing pottery dated to the 12th century and a yard dating to the 14th century were found. Also in Peckham High Street, at **Eagle Wharf**, tile and pottery dating to the medieval period were found but no structural remains. These were probably garden features belonging to the medieval manor house. In **Camberwell Green** archaeologists found carved stone that had come from nearby medieval buildings.

The Canterbury Tales

Bifel that in that seson on a day,
In Southwerk at the Tabard as I lay
Redy to wenden on my pilgrymage
To Caunterbury with ful devout corage,
At nyght was come into that hostelrye
Wel nyne and twenty in a compaignye,
Of sondry folk, by aventure yfalle
In felawshipe, and pilgrimes were they alle,
That toward Caunterbury wolden ryde.
The chambres and the stables weren wyde,
And wel we weren esed atte beste.

Chaucer, from the *Prologue*

Hamo holds Camberwell himself. Norman held it from King Edward [the Confessor].
Then it answered for 12 hides, now for 6 hides and 1 virgate.
Land for 5 ploughs. In lordship 2;
22 villagers and 7 smallholders with 6 ploughs. A church.
Meadow, 63 acres; woodland at 60 pigs.
Value before 1066, £12; later £6; now £14.

The Bishop of Lisieux holds Peckham from the Bishop. Aefled held it from Harold before 1066. It lay in [the lands of] Battersea.
Then and now it answered for 2 hides. Land for 1 plough.
1 villager and 3 smallholders.
Meadow, 2 acres.
Value before 1066 and now 30s; when acquired 20s.

Baynard holds Walworth from the Archbishop. Before 1066 it was for the clothing of the monks. Then it answered for 5 hides;
now for $3^1/_2$ hides. Land for 3 ploughs. In lordship 1 plough;
14 villagers and 5 smallholders with 3 ploughs. A church.
Meadow, 8 acres.
Value before 1066, 30s; later 20s; now 60s.

translated from *Domesday Book*

The standing remains of Winchester Palace. Parts of the palace survived as warehouses and tenements which were destroyed by fire in 1814 revealing the original walls of the Great Hall and service range

Portrait of Sir John Fastolf (1378–1459). A soldier in the wars of Henry V and Henry VI, he was accused of cowardice at the battle of Patay in 1429 and appears in Shakespeare's Henry VI part 1 (although Shakespeare's Falstaff in later plays is not based on him). Letters from him and about him survive among the documents known as the 'Paston Letters' – one of the earliest surviving collections of family letters in English (most of them now in the British Library)

Royals and nobles

Southwark's proximity to both the City of London and the royal court at Westminster made it an ideal place for nobles and great churchmen to build their town houses. The London residence of the bishops of Winchester until the 17th century was Winchester Palace. It was constructed in the 12th century by Bishop Henry de Blois, King Stephen's brother, because of 'the many inconveniences and losses sustained through the lack of a house of our own when called to London on royal or other business'. Part of the great hall of Winchester Palace with its 14th-century rose window can be seen in **Clink Street**.

Two medieval kings built residences in Southwark, easily reached by the river from Westminster. *La Rosere*, or the Rosary, was constructed by Edward II in 1325, and in 1353–61 Edward III had another moated house built at **Platform Wharf** in Rotherhithe.

The Rosary

On the site of **London Bridge City** on **Tooley Street**, in 1987–8, archaeologists found stone foundations, floors and yards of the Rosary precinct surrounded by a moat. Edward II was murdered in 1327, and it is unclear from documentary sources whether the house remained a royal residence. The Rosary estate was acquired in 1446 by Sir John Fastolf who built a new moated house near the Rosary, known as Fastolf's Place.

Part of an elaborate oak-panelled door from the house, made in the early 15th century, was reused to support the sides of the moat. In the moat there was a three-sided timber tank internally braced to resist pressure from outside. It may have been a storage tank for fish or eels. Tiny bones of cod and ray were found on the excavation.

The wall of the Rosary before the new development of London Bridge City

Edward III's house

Another royal mansion was built further downstream at the former **Platform Wharf**, **Bermondsey Wall East**, near the medieval riverside village of **Rotherhithe**. Here Edward III constructed a moated mansion, perhaps to replace his father's Rosary as the king's occasional residence in Southwark. Archaeologists found remains of stone walls, standing up to 3 metres high, surrounded by a moat nearly 8 metres wide.

Platform Wharf cesspit

Edward's manor contained a hall, a kitchen, the King's Chamber and possibly his chapel and other chambers. Archaeologists found a privy and a tower at the north-west corner of the building, projecting out over the moat, as well as three stone-lined cesspits. In some cases along the waterfront medieval privies emptied directly into the river. The pits were cleaned out every few years by breaking open the masonry around the top. The site of Edward III's manor house can be visited next door to **The Angel** pub, where some of the medieval walls can be seen.

Some of the walls of the Inner Court of Edward III's manor house are now on display

Monasteries in medieval Southwark

Little remains of the parish churches of medieval Southwark – most have been rebuilt or destroyed – but there were two great monasteries which have been investigated by archaeologists.

Priory of St Mary Overie

The Augustinian priory church of St Mary Overy was largely rebuilt as the Cathedral Church of St Saviour and St Mary Overy Southwark by the Victorians, but much of the 13th- and 14th-century church survives. The priory was founded about 1106 and dissolved by Henry VIII in 1539. The name St Mary Overy (or St Mary over-the-rie) derives from the church's location 'over the river' from the City. In **Montague Close**, part of the priory buildings to the east of the main monastic cloister were found, together with a stone-lined well of 14th-century date and a number of rubbish pits. One of the pits contained human bones, which may have come from a nearby burial ground. To the north of **Southwark Cathedral** archaeologists have recently found more masonry, probably part of the cloister.

Southwark Cathedral

Fragments of medieval walls of the priory at St Mary Overy

Photo © Pre-Construct Archaeology

Abbey of St Saviour (Bermondsey Abbey)

The abbey of St Saviour was located on **Bermondsey island**, surrounded by marshland. It was probably built on the site of an earlier Saxon minster church and was founded here in 1089 by Cluniac monks from France. Queen Elizabeth Woodville, widow of Edward IV, was forced to retire to the abbey by her son-in-law, Henry VII. She died there five years later, in 1492.

The abbey was dissolved in 1538 and the abbey church demolished shortly afterwards. The abbey's remains lie mostly beneath modern **Abbey Street** at its junction with **Tower Bridge Road**. Archaeological excavations on the south side of Abbey Street have located the monastic frater (refectory) and dorter (dormitory), a chapel, the infirmary (hospital) and reredorter (latrine). Part of the precinct wall of the abbey was found buried just below the modern pavement level. It survived because it was incorporated into an Elizabethan brick-built cellar. Walls and floors of the abbey have been found under the **Bermondsey antiques market**.

Bermondsey antiques market on a Friday morning. The market area is located within a courtyard to the west of the church of Bermondsey Abbey. Bermondsey Street marks the western precinct wall of the abbey

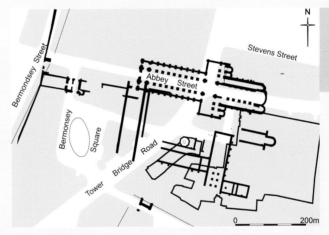

The layout of Bermondsey Abbey beneath Abbey Street

A souvenir badge depicting the Rood (crucifix) of Bermondsey found in 1992 by archaeologists near Tower Bridge, but only identified in 1999. The letters on the labels either side of Christ seem to be Latin for 'this is the badge of Bermondsey'. The actual Rood probably dated to the Saxon period and is said to have been discovered near the abbey in 1117. It became a focus of pilgrimage in the medieval period. The badge of lead and tin would have been bought by a pilgrim visiting the shrine. Only two others are known – one in the Netherlands

Medieval hospitals

In addition to the monastic infirmaries there were other hospitals in medieval Southwark, including a leper hospital that once stood near the junction of **Great Dover Street** and the **Old Kent Road**. The plans of medieval hospitals are unknown but they probably looked like the monastic infirmaries from which they were derived. The most famous medieval hospital in Southwark was dedicated to St Thomas Becket and was built in the early 13th century. Part of the undercroft of the medieval chapel belonging to the hospital was found by archaeologists in **St Thomas Street**. The hospital moved to a new riverside site in Lambeth in 1871 to make way for the railway extension to Charing Cross.

Shakespeare's Southwark

During the medieval period the Bankside area of Southwark was famous for its many brothels popularly known as the 'stewes', as well as gambling and drinking dens. **Park Street** was once called Maiden Lane, which probably refers ironically to the prostitutes of Bankside. In the 16th and 17th centuries the area developed as an entertainment centre. These activities were prohibited within the City of London but flourished in the less strictly regulated area of **Bankside**, which could be reached either on foot over London Bridge or by boat across the river.

Bearbaiting

Other 'low-life' activities included bear- and bullbaiting, which were a major form of entertainment in the 16th and 17th centuries . Betting, challenges and wagers were part of the excitement and bearbaiting was a favourite spectator sport for the monarchy. Five bearbaiting arenas are thought to have existed in the area of **Bankside** and **Park Street**.

Archaeologists uncovered the timber piles underlying robbed-out wall foundations of a bearbaiting arena at **Benbow House** in **Bear Gardens**, a narrow lane that runs between Park Street and Bankside. They also found dog bones – possibly remains of the mastiffs – and horse bones which showed signs of butchery and gnawing indicating that these bones had been fed to the mastiffs. Two bones from a European brown bear were found during excavation of the **Rose Theatre** site and were probably from the nearby bearbaiting arenas. Two bear skeletons were found in a pit nearby at **Skinmarket Place** and were probably more casualties of the sport.

Bear- and bullbaiting in Germany from a woodcut of 1689. Bears were chained to a central stake and attacked by mastiffs

A description of one of the bearbaiting arenas has been left by Paul Hentzner, a German who visited it in 1598.

[The arena is] built in the form of a theatre, which serves for the baiting of bulls and bears; they are fastened behind, and then worried by great English bull-dogs, but not without great risk to the dogs, from the horns of the one, and the teeth of the other; and it sometimes happens they are killed upon the spot; fresh ones are immediately supplied in the place of those that are wounded, or tired. To this entertainment, there often follows that of whipping a blinded bear, which is performed by five or six men, standing circularly with whips, which they exercise upon him without any mercy, as he cannot escape from them because of his chain; he defends himself with all his force and skill, throwing down all who come within his reach, and are not active enough to get out of it, and tearing the whips out of their hands, and breaking them. At these spectacles, and everywhere else, the English are constantly smoking tobacco ... fruits, such as apples, pears and nuts, according to the season, are carried about to be sold, as well as wine and ale.

Paul Hentzner's Travels in England, translated by Richard Bentley, 1797

This early 17th-century painting of the Anglo-Dutch school, based on earlier panoramas, looks towards the City from Southwark. The flag-flying theatres are clearly visible to the west of Southwark Cathedral, but the shape of the theatres is misleading – archaeological evidence confirms that they were circular

One of the most famous actors of the day, Edward Alleyn, became Master of the Royal Game of Bears, Bulls and Dogs in 1604. Among his many roles he played the leads in first performances of Christopher Marlowe's *Doctor Faustus* and *Tamburlaine*, and Shakespeare's *Henry VI*, at the Rose Theatre.

Sometimes the Bear Gardens housed more exotic animals. In 1611 Alleyn had two white bears and a lion. There were also ponies, apes and bulls. The Puritans unsuccessfully tried to end bearbaiting in the 1650s. The High Sheriff of Surrey, Thomas Pride, signed a notice declaring:

The Bear Baiting and playing for Prizes ... hitherto practised in Southwark ... which have caused great Evills and Abominations, [are] to be suppressed from this time.

Edward Alleyn made a fortune in the theatre and founded Dulwich College, in south Southwark, where he is buried

The Bankside playhouses

The animal-baiting arenas possibly influenced the style of the open-air playhouses that were built in Southwark towards the end of the 16th century. There were four on **Bankside**. The two most famous are the Rose and the Globe – where many of Shakespeare's plays were first performed. Both playhouses have recently been found by archaeologists. The Hope has also now been located on the east side of **Bear Gardens**. The Swan is known only from documents and old maps and there is little chance that any of it survives.

The archaeological excavation at the Rose Theatre in 1989

The Rose Theatre

The Rose was the first purpose-built open-air theatre on **Bankside**. It was built in 1587 for Philip Henslowe, who became Edward Alleyn's father-in-law. Alleyn placed Henslowe's papers and diary in **Dulwich College** library, and these records provide much of the history of the Rose.

Despite the popularity and importance of the playhouses in the development of English drama, very little was known of their structure or design. The archaeological investigation of the Rose in 1988–9 has now provided the first detailed information.

Leather shoe from excavations at the Rose Theatre

The archaeological excavation was conducted before the construction of a new office block now called **Rose Court**. Archaeologists uncovered much of the ground plan of the Rose and two phases of construction were clearly visible, although much remains to be discovered. The first building appears to have been 14-sided with two parallel foundations 3.5 metres apart built of chalk and brick. The timber frame sat on the foundations and formed the main supports for the gallery seating which encircled an open, central yard, or pit. The yard floor was mortared and sloped down towards the stage. This was where the groundlings stood, paying the cheapest entrance fee. The area in front of the stage had been worn away, possibly by the feet of people crowding to the stage front.

Money box tops found at the Rose, shown with a complete example.

Gatherers were stationed at the doors to collect entrance fees. At the Rose, archaeologists found a large number of broken money boxes – pottery jars with distinctive coin slots near their top knob handle.

At the Rose Theatre archaeologists found hazelnut shells which probably formed part of the yard

A gold ring found during excavations of the second yard surface of the Rose. The motto on the ring is in French and translates as 'Think of me, God willing'

An assortment of pins found at the Rose

Substantial alterations took place at the Rose in 1592, mainly to the northern half of the building and the stage area, which was pushed north to create more space in the yard. A new yard floor was laid; it was a mixture of dark brown silt and slag (probably fuel waste). There was also a quantity of broken hazelnut shells. This was possibly industrial waste rather then food refuse.

The Rose was probably three storeys high and when rebuilt in 1592 could have held over 2000 people, including those standing in the yard area. The large audience and the enclosed nature of the theatre would have made for intimate performances, no doubt with plenty of audience participation. There were occasional closures due to outbreaks of the plague or, as in June 1595, because of riots in Southwark's market. By about 1606 it was no longer in use.

Archaeologists' discovery of the Rose Theatre was reported around the world. The extent, quality and significance of the Rose remains became apparent towards the end of the period of excavation. Construction work for the new offices had already commenced on part of the site but there was enormous pressure from MPs, actors, theatre historians, archaeologists and local people to protect the remains. After much discussion a compromise was reached which included a redesign of the proposed basement area of the new office block. This allowed sufficient space to enable the theatre remains to be saved and displayed to the public at a future date. An exhibition at the site in **Park Street** opened in April 1999.

Actors' protest wins reprieve for the Rose

Builders blocked for one month

Press cuttings of the discovery of the Rose in 1989

Actors pledge to maintain vigil

£1 million grant to halt building on Rose Theatre

By George Jones and Nigel Reynolds

THE GOVERNMENT stepped in yesterday to halt building work on the site of the historic Rose Theatre in Southwark, south London, for 28 days to enable agreement to be reached on a way to preserve the remains of the stage where Shakespeare once performed.

The Swan Theatre

The Swan has been located in the area of **Hopton Street** near Blackfriars Bridge. It has not been investigated by archaeologists but is known from documents, including a copy of a drawing dated to around 1596, possibly the year in which it was built, which showed what the interior of the theatre looked like.

The Swan was the scene of one of the great scandals of theatrical history. In 1597 a subversive play (now lost) written by Ben Jonson and Thomas Nashe and other actors, called *The Isle of Dogs*, was perfomed at the Swan. The play was described as containing 'very seditious and slanderous matter' and 'leude and mutynous behaviour'. Ben Jonson was jailed; Nashe fled; and it seems all the public playhouses were closed for sometime.

Excavations at the Globe

The Globe Theatre

The Globe became the leading theatre of the day and was the venue for the first performances of Shakespeare's tragedies *Hamlet, Macbeth, Othello* and *King Lear*. It was built in 1599, very near the Rose, from the dismantled timber framework of the Theatre in Shoreditch. In 1989 archaeologists found a small part of its chalk and brick foundations.

On 29 June 1613 Shakespeare's *Henry VIII* was being performed when, following the discharge of a cannon, the Globe caught fire and burned down. Sir Henry Wotton, poet, diplomat and theatregoer, described the fire in a letter (although he may not have been an eyewitness).

where being thought at first but an idle smoke, and their eyes more attentive to the show, it kindled inwardly [in the thatch] and ran round like a train, consuming within less than an hour the whole house to the very ground.

Front and back views of some of the Tudor coins found at the Rose Theatre site

Within a year, the company of shareholders rebuilt the theatre in brick, timber and plaster, a tiled roof replacing the original thatch where the fire had started.

As with the remains of the Rose, the Globe was protectively covered and the site was designated a Scheduled Ancient Monument (that is, protected by law). The edge of the two bays that were excavated are now marked by coloured cobbles in the courtyard of **Old Theatre Court** off **Park Street**, where there are information boards about the archaeologists' discoveries.

The American actor and director Sam Wanamaker (1919–93) had an ambition to rebuild the Globe Theatre as near as possible to the original site and to the original design, although there were very few documents or maps available. The ground plan and design were changed following the 1989 archaeological discoveries at the Rose and the Globe. The reconstructed Globe opened in 1997 with Shakespeare's *Henry V*.

The new Globe theatre was built with traditional materials and techniques. The architects were Theo Crosby and Jon Greenfield, and the master craftsman was Peter McCurdy

Portrait of Shakespeare – this detail comes from a commemmoration plaque on Park Street, on the site of the original Globe Theatre

> But pardon, gentles all,
> The flat unraised spirits that hath dared
> On this unworthy scaffold* to bring forth
> So great an object. Can this cockpit hold
> The vasty fields of France? Or may we cram
> Within this wooden O* the very casques
> That did affright the air at Agincourt?
>
> Shakespeare, *Henry V*, Chorus
>
> *   'scaffold' – the playhouse stage
>   'wooden O' – probably the Globe Theatre

The Hope Theatre

In 1999 archaeologists found a small part of the brick foundations of what might have been the Hope Theatre underneath a car park on the east side of **Bear Gardens** lane. The foundations were buried 3 metres down.

Philip Henslowe had the old bearbaiting arena at **Bear Gardens** demolished in 1613 and built a new theatre named the Hope, which was modelled on the Swan. The Hope was unique among the London playhouses in being used for a dual purpose: for animal-baiting and for the performance of plays. The stage was removable and set on trestles. A bricklayer, John Browne, stated in 1620 that Henslowe

did begin to lay the foundacion of the new playhouse uppon part of the old beare garden, and that afterwards he did alter part of the foundacion thereof and sett it in the place where it now standeth, and that Mr Edward Allens perswasion did move and induce him soe to doe, because he should sett the foundacion thereof wholly upon the Kinges lande, and did sett the foundacion thereof about foure foot further southward uppon the Kinges landes then it was first laid.

The building could have been a timber-framed construction placed upon brick foundations, which were put in by John Browne at a cost of £80. Bear- and bullbaiting were carried out on Mondays and the rest of the week was used for plays, which began at 3pm.

Henslowe died in 1616 leaving the running of the Hope to his partner who concentrated more on animal-baiting than the performance of plays. From now on the Hope was commonly called the 'Bear-Baiting House' and no major plays were performed.

The author cleaning the brick foundations of the Hope Theatre in Bear Gardens

In 1655 following the attempted Puritan suppression of bearbaiting, seven bears were shot on the orders of Thomas Pride, High Sheriff of Surrey, by a company of soldiers outside the Hope. A year later the Hope was pulled down by Thomas Walker, a Petticoat Maker from Cannon Street, who built tenements on the site.

Industry in post-medieval Southwark

From Tudor times up to the 18th century, Southwark became increasingly industrialised, and was home to many industries which, because of their dangerous or noisy nature, were excluded by legislation from the City. Other trades flourished as a direct result of Southwark's riverside location. Recent excavations have provided evidence for some of these industries and a few examples are described below.

Tanning

Tanner Street, Morocco Street, Leathermarket Street: as its street names show, one of Bermondsey's principal industries was leatherworking. From medieval times until well into the 20th century Bermondsey was the main centre of leather production in England. It was ideally situated for the development of a leather industry as it could obtain a ready supply of skins from the butchers of London, and was close to the principal market for its produce. The various processes of tanning required huge quantities of water, and Bermondsey had an ample supply in the numerous tidal streams and artificial ditches by which this low-lying district was drained.

Leatherworks at Bevingtons' Neckinger Leather Mills in Grange Road in 1862. Half a million cured skins a year were produced here.
Southwark Local Studies Library

Tanning was the treatment of cattle hides by immersion in a solution of vegetable tannin (usually oak bark) to produce a heavy-duty leather for use by shoemakers and saddlers. The tanning of cattle hides took place in large, timber-lined pits and took many months. Another process, tawing, was much faster and was used principally for treating the skins of smaller animals such as sheep, goats, calves and pigs.

Underneath the yard of the old Sarson's Vinegar factory on **Tanner Street** archaeologists found wooden casks set into pits and filled with slaked lime dating to the 17th century. They would have been too small to contain a complete cow hide but could have accommodated sheep skins; many leg bones of sheep were found in pits and in a silted-up pond indicating that tawing was the main practice. Leather shoes with tassels attached were found.

The site continued in use as a tanyard until the second half of the 18th century. At this time large plank-lined tanks for tanning cattle hides were constructed. One of these was equipped with a lead drainpipe, for discharging spent tanning solution into the adjacent roadside ditch.

Tanning pits found under the yard of Sarson's Vinegar factory

Sarson's Vinegar factory, Bermondsey

South London dominated the development of vinegar brewing and became the main production centre in Britain. Sarson's Vinegar factory buildings (1814–1992) were recorded by archaeologists. After planning permission was given for conversion of the building, archaeologists drew and photographed the building and interviewed local residents who had worked at the plant. This will ensure that a record of the factory and vinegar brewing processes is preserved.

More tanning pits have been found recently to the south of Tanner Street along **Tower Bridge Road**. These were made in the 18th and 19th centuries from planks, and contained horse, cattle and sheep bones of animals used in the tanning industry here.

Tanning and tawing

Hides were delivered to the tannery with the horns and sometimes the hooves attached. These were trimmed off and the hides washed. The hair and flesh were loosened, usually by immersing the hides in pits containing a solution of lime, and the hides scraped. To remove excess lime and to make the hides softer they were soaked in an alkaline solution of bird droppings or dog dung (puering), or were immersed in an acidic solution of rye, barley or ash bark (drenching).

The hides were then soaked in pits containing increasingly concentrated tannin solution. During this process, which could take up to a year, the tannins combined chemically with the skins in an irreversible process that made them waterproof and rot-resistant.

Once the hides were tanned they were smoothed out and hung to dry and then passed to curriers, whose job it was to shave the hides to a uniform thickness.

In tawing a combination of alum and other substances such as egg yolk, oil, butter or flour was worked into the skin, to produce a lighter leather for the manufacture of gloves, most leather garments, laces and shoe uppers. Traditionally the tawyer did this by trampling the skin with bare feet in a tub set on the ground. Morocco leather was made from goat skins using sumac, a type of bark.

Cross-sections through the tanning pits can be seen behind the archaeologist

Shipbuilding and shipbreaking

Much of London's shipbuilding and shipping trade was carried out within **Rotherhithe** and **Bermondsey**. There were at least 12 major shipyards in Rotherhithe, as well as yards for barge-building and shipbreaking.

Part of a shipbuilding yard was excavated at Bellamy's Wharf 40 metres to the south of today's riverfront and just to the east of the old Surrey canal, now **Surrey Water**. Burnt remains of large ships, possibly from the first or second Dutch War, were reused to make a dock and river wall in the 1660s.

Cleaning the carved knighthead – a vertical timber on the deck through which the rigging ropes pass – from a large 17th-century ship at Bellamy's Wharf

17th-century ships' timbers at Bellamy's Wharf reused as land ties for a dock inlet and river wall. The curved white-lead painted timber is a virtually complete stem (the main upright timber at the bow of the ship) from a large ship very similar to that of the Vasa, a complete, Swedish ocean-going warship built in 1624 and now on display in Stockholm

The dock was constructed of posts set in baseplates to which timber planking was nailed. There were timber tiebacks to secure the posts. Some ship timbers were also reused within the foundations of 18th- and 19th-century buildings.

One shipbreaking yard was on **Rotherhithe Street** close to **Bellamy's Wharf**. In the 1830s the yard was occupied by a shipbreaker called John Beatson who broke up the *Temeraire*. This old warship was a veteran of the Battle of Trafalgar in 1805. In 1838 the elderly J M W Turner painted the ship being towed by a small tug to the yard to be broken up. It was a favourite painting of his (now at the National Gallery, London). Some of the ship's timbers went to make two bishops' chairs and a communion table for **St Paul's Church** off Rotherhithe Street and are now in **St Mary's Church**, Rotherhithe.

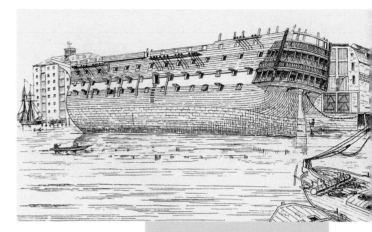

John Beatson's drawing of the Temeraire beached at Rotherhithe in 1838

River trading

Ship timbers were also reused to build revetments in the 16th century at **Adlards Wharf** on **Bermondsey Wall West**. Along with the revetments, archaeologists also found a slipway leading into the river and a crane base. At **Spice Quay** near **Butler's Wharf**, archaeologists found large dumps of 16th- and 17th-century rubbish which had been placed on top of the riverbank to reclaim the land. The rubbish had been contained within timber revetments.

A whaling station dating to the 18th century was excavated on the south side of **Greenland Dock** at **Rainbow Quay**. Archaeologists found a circular brick base for a large copper vessel in which whale blubber would have been boiled. To one side was a sunken timber tank for collecting the blubber residue or fenk. This was clearly a processing centre for extracting whale oil for lamps and soapmaking. Two huge whale bones from the Greenland Right whale were found – this was the main whale hunted in northern Europe – hence the name Greenland Dock.

A blubber rendering furnace and attached chimney base of the whaling station at Rainbow Quay

Photo © Thames Valley Archaeology Service

Clay pipemaking

Smoking a clay pipe in the early 19th century

Guildhall Library, Corporation of London

Tobacco was introduced to England in the 1570s by travellers from the New World. They had adopted the habit of smoking the dried leaves, for their supposed medicinal qualities, from the American Indians.

The style of clay tobacco pipes changed considerably during the three hundred years in which they were in popular usage. The earliest pipes were mostly plain and undecorated, although some were marked with the maker's initials or symbol. From the 18th century pipe bowls began to be decorated with moulded designs such as plumes of ostrich feathers, royal or company coats of arms, and Masonic emblems – symbols associated with the Freemasons such as compasses and dividers. The great age of the decorated pipe was the 19th century: designs included public house signs, political slogans and even portraits or caricatures of prominent Victorians.

A 17th-century pipemaker's workshop was discovered in **Borough High Street**. The remains of two brick-built kilns were found, served by a single stoking pit. Nearby were two pits for storing or processing clay, and another pit, probably for storing coal. The clay muffle (the domed superstructure within which the pipes were stacked for firing), had collapsed into the interior of one of the kilns. Enough of the muffle survived for this kiln to be reconstructed, and it is now displayed in the Museum of London.

It is possible that the workshop found in Borough High Street was operated by the Blundell family of pipemakers, who are known to have been in the area from at least 1682 and who were still working there in the 18th century. The picture shows Henry Blundell's pipes decorated with the Royal Arms of the House of Hanover (on the left) and the Arms of the Company of Watermen (on the right)

Potteries

Pottery was produced in Southwark from the medieval period. However, the area is known primarily for the production of London delftware in the 17th and 18th centuries. Delftware, or tin-glazed earthenware, was first made in London at the Aldgate factory in 1571, some 30 years before it was produced in the Dutch city of Delft from which it derives its popular name.

Out of 19 known delftware factories in the London area, eight were in north Southwark. The first two were at **Montague Close**, established in 1613, and **Pickleherring** (which stood near today's Southwark Crown Court) around 1616. Archaeologists found part of the kiln at **Montague Close** during digging on the north side of **Southwark Cathedral**. This will be preserved and put on public display in a new building.

The delftware kiln at Montague Close
Photo © Pre-Construct Archaeology

Pickleherring pothouse

Thomas Townsend was recorded as running the Pickleherring pothouse in 1638. He does not appear to have managed his affairs in a particularly organised fashion. Between 1631 and 1641 he was fined for multiple transgressions including having a false four-pound weight, keeping hogs, dumping soil in a channel, not maintaining the pavement, not cleaning his sewer and drain, dumping sand and gravel in the highway, not paving the ground and putting up a fence which partially blocked the highway.

Delftware wall tiles found at former Platform Wharf, Paradise Street

Another delftware factory was established at the former **Platform Wharf, Paradise Street** in **Rotherhithe**, in about 1638, by Thomas Barnebowe, in what had once been Edward III's moated manor house. Two brick-built kilns were found in the house. The walls of the house had been refaced in brick, and windows, doors and the privies were blocked. The moat was drained and infilled, largely with waste from the pottery factory. This included huge quantities of unglazed (biscuit-fired) pots, complete painted and glazed vessels, and internal fittings and lining material from the kilns. The industry is preserved in the name of nearby **Pottery Street**.

Biscuit-ware salts in the form of figurines from the Montague Close pothouse. The seated figures hold shallow dishes in which salt would have been placed for use at the table

Glassmaking

There have been a number of glassworks in Southwark, located principally in the **Bankside** area. One of these was the Falcon Glassworks established in 1814 by Apsley Pellatt. Archaeologists found the glasshouse furnace and many bowls, phials and lamps. There was an earlier glasshouse underneath dating to the mid 1700s.

John Bowles and John Lillington set up a factory at **Bear Gardens** in 1671, on the site of an earlier glassworks. Here they specialised in the manufacture of crown window glass – made by spinning a gather of glass on the end of a rod so that it spread into a large disc, which could then be cut into pieces for windows. Archaeologists found extensive dumps of glass including mirror and vessel glass and glasshouse waste such as furnace bricks and crucible fragments.

The 18th-century furnace at the Falcon Glassworks. The large wall at the back is part of the 19th-century glasshouse of Apsley Pellat III

Photo © Pre-Construct Archaeology

Waterworks and waterpipes

Just downstream from the **Design Museum** at **Jacob's Island**, **Jacob Street**, archaeologists found that the mill stream belonging to St Saviour's mill had been revetted with timber to keep the sides from collapse. The stream was filled with black sticky clay containing numerous finds dating from the 17th to the 19th century including leather, pottery, clay tobacco pipes and glass, and a number of metal objects including furniture mounts and cutlery. This was the domestic rubbish thrown into the stream from the overhanging houses.

During the 18th century, waterworks were established to serve local industries such as the tanning works. A brick and timber channel and silt trap which ran into an arch-vaulted brick drain were found during the excavation.

Near to that part of the Thames on which the church at Rotherhithe abuts, where the buildings on the banks are dirtiest and the vessels on the river blackest with the dust of colliers and the smoke of close-built low-roofed houses, there exists, at the present day, the filthiest, the strangest, the most extraordinary of the many localities that are hidden in London, wholly unknown, even by name, to the great mass of its inhabitants.

... In such a neighbourhood, beyond Dockhead in the Borough of Southwark, stands Jacob's Island, surrounded by a muddy ditch, six or eight feet deep and fifteen or twenty wide when the tide is in, once called Mill Pond.

Charles Dickens, *Oliver Twist*, revised 1846, chapter 50

The excavations at Jacob's Island. On the right are the timbers from the sides of the 17th-century mill stream. On the left are the brick-lined channel and silt trap of the 18th-century waterworks

Watercolour of Jacob's Island painted in 1887 by J. Stewart showing the mill stream and dilapidated buildings

To the west of **St Saviour's dock** archaeologists found evidence of another local Southwark industry. The Hay's Wharf Company was founded in 1651 and was one of the largest wharf companies. The official name of **Hay's Wharf** became 'Pipe Boarers Wharf'. Here wooden water pipes were made from hollowed-out tree trunks, usually elm, and some of these were found at the excavation in **Tooley Street**.

The trunk was placed on a trestle and bored by the use of a large wooden handle which turned an auger or drill. One end of the trunk was tapered and at the other end the bore was enlarged so that the pipes could be fitted together. The lifespan of the pipes was short as the ends tended to split – they could last up to 25 years but were usually replaced before this. Wooden water pipes went out of fashion and were replaced by iron water pipes towards the end of the 18th century.

Archaeologists find elm pipes of the mid to late 18th century

The pipe borer in use

Transport in the 19th century

The building of canals was of great advantage to the market gardeners on the outskirts of the built-up area. The Surrey Canal Company was formed in 1801 and work started on the canal from **Rotherhithe** to the **Kent Road** in 1802, and Kent Road to **Camberwell** in 1803. The Camberwell entrance to **Burgess Park** was once the western end of the **Grand Surrey Canal**, which was drained in 1960 and later infilled. There was an extension to the canal as far as **Canal Head** close to **Peckham High Street** which was reached in 1826. Archaeologists found the canal wall during an excavation at Canal Head, Peckham. The canal itself had been infilled with layers of building rubble and sand.

Part of the brick-built kiln in Burgess Park used for lime burning to make cement in the 19th century

The canals were used to transport coal, timber and building materials and market garden produce. Other industries, such as lime burning, grew up with the arrival of the canals. The remains of a brick-built lime kiln can still be seen in **Burgess Park**. It was part of the limeworks of E R Burtt and Sons who worked there from 1816 to the 1960s. The limeworks were used to heat limestone to convert into quicklime for cement.

Up until the 1800s the rural part of south Southwark was largely open space with scattered farms and hamlets at **Peckham, Nunhead, Camberwell** and **Dulwich**. These villages also had their upmarket areas where large houses were built for the wealthy. In the Victorian period, 1837–1901, major changes took place due to the expansion in manufacturing and industry, and much of the land was built upon.

The building of the railways began in the early part of the 19th century and lines were built down to **Greenwich** and to Dover and Brighton via **West Dulwich** and **Peckham**. **Nunhead** was one of the stations on a high-level railway that ran to **Crystal Palace**. This was closed in 1954 but has now been reopened as a pleasant walkway. Part of the tunnels and footbridge still remain at **Cox's Walk** at the northern entrance to **Dulwich** and **Sydenham Hill Woods**.

This period also saw the construction of new roads and tramlines, and in 1890 the Underground came to Southwark from **London Bridge** to the **Elephant and Castle**.

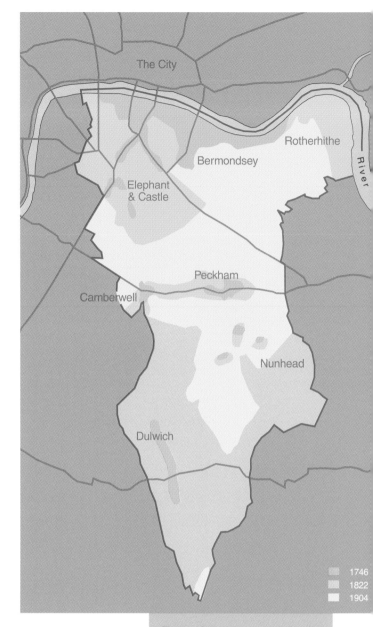

The spread of suburbia through the 18th and 19th centuries

1746
1822
1904

The Old Crystal Palace high-level railway

The preservation of Southwark's past

Reconciling progress with preservation is difficult. Almost all developments disturb – and destroy – archaeological remains. Archaeology is about preserving the past, but it is also about development and change. Archaeological remains are the physical history of thousands of years of development. They show us how each generation of Southwark residents has taken the environment their predecessors created and changed it to meet their own needs. Archaeology teaches us that urban regeneration cannot stop if a city is to thrive, but it shows us too that we must take account of the past when shaping the Southwark of the new millennium.

The rate of commercial redevelopment and building in Southwark over the last 50 years has created a need for both amateur and professional archaeological teams. These archaeologists have worked in parallel with the process of development and regeneration to preserve and record Southwark's history.

In partnership with the London Borough of Southwark, English Heritage and the London Docklands Development Corporation, archaeologists have tried to ensure that we do not build the Southwark of the future at the expense of the past.

The future seems very bright for Southwark. The arrival of the **Jubilee Line Extension** now connects much of north Southwark with its dockland heritage. The **Design Museum** and the new **Globe Theatre** already form major attractions and the **Millennium Bridge**, the **Tate Gallery of Modern Art** at Bankside, **Vinopolis** (the wine museum) will promote tourism, and will create a rich environment that people are proud to live and work in. These projects will bring new archaeological finds to light. They will help us write new chapters in the story of Southwark.

The new Tate Gallery of Modern Art

Where to find out more

Southwark has many places of interest to visit, such as the remains of the Great Hall of Winchester Palace in **Clink Street**, Edward III's moated house in **Rotherhithe**, the site of the Rose Theatre in **Park Street** and the exhibition on Shakespeare at the new **Globe Theatre**.

The public are able to see the results of archaeological investigation in the galleries of the **Museum of London, London Wall**. Over the last few years new galleries on prehistoric and Roman London have opened, incorporating the best of the recent discoveries including the Roman painted wall plaster from Winchester Palace. There are also a number of museums in Southwark, such as the **Cuming Museum** on **Walworth Road** which has many archaeological finds.

The **Local Studies Library** opposite **Borough tube station** has many pamphlets and books of interest, including the London Borough of Southwark's Neighbourhood History series and other local history books. The library also has various leaflets of historic walks, for example around **Rotherhithe** to view old buildings and places of interest, and the walk along the **Crystal Palace** (high-level) railway. The **Southwark Tourist Information Centre** at **London Bridge** also provides information and leaflets.

There are local groups based in Southwark such as the **Southwark and Lambeth Archaeological Society**. Training courses are offered at Birkbeck College of the University of London. Students attend a training archaeological excavation which takes place in Southwark in the summer.

Training digs in Lant Street and Lafone Street, Southwark, 1999